T0162861

Shrii Prabhat Ranjan Sarkar

Shrii Prabhat Ranjan Sarkar

Beacon of Hope for Suffering Humanity

Garda Ghista

authorHOUSE®

AuthorHouse™
1663 Liberty Drive
Bloomington, IN 47403
www.authorhouse.com
Phone: 1-800-839-8640

© *2011 Garda Ghista. All rights reserved.*

*No part of this book may be reproduced, stored in
a retrieval system, or transmitted by any means
without the written permission of the author.*

First published by AuthorHouse 01/18/2011

ISBN: 978-1-4567-1531-1 (sc)
ISBN: 978-1-4567-1530-4 (e-b)

Printed in the United States of America

*Any people depicted in stock imagery provided by Thinkstock are models,
and such images are being used for illustrative purposes only.
Certain stock imagery © Thinkstock.*

This book is printed on acid-free paper.

*Because of the dynamic nature of the Internet, any Web addresses or
links contained in this book may have changed since publication and
may no longer be valid. The views expressed in this work are solely those
of the author and do not necessarily reflect the views of the publisher,
and the publisher hereby disclaims any responsibility for them.*

Contents

Dedication

Shrii Prabhat Ranjan Sarkar said, "Tell everyone that 'I am yours'... I love each and every particle of this universe."

Shrii Sarkar also said, 'I want that you go to the place where there is the maximum suffering. The convenience of the people there comes first. The convenience of others comes second. And your convenience comes last."

Hence this book is dedicated to all the oppressed people of the world.

You will bring about a radical change in the social order so that each individual can find ample scope for physical, mental and spiritual evolution. Remove the sorrow and suffering of exploited humanity; wipe the tears from their eyes. Build an ideal human society based on dharma. Let this be the sole mission of your life.

Shrii Prabhat Ranjan Sarkar

Shrii Prabhat Ranjan Sarkar

Early Years

Shrii Prabhat Ranjan Sarkar was born on May 21st, 1921 in Jamalpur, a small town in the rural part of northern India in the state of Bihar. Astrologers who took his horoscope proclaimed that he would vanquish all religions and establish his own universal dharma on earth. When he was nine years old, religious fundamentalists who heard of this prediction tried to kill him, but failed. Yet Shrii Sarkar never expressed any hatred or religious animosity. On the contrary, he propagated only neohumanistic love for everyone.

He was the eldest son of two sisters and three brothers. His father was a renowned homeopathic doctor in Jamalpur. After attending college in Kolkata during the early war years, Shrii Sarkar took employment with the auditing department of the Jamalpur railway workshop in 1944. By that time he had embarked on his mission as a preceptor of Tantric spiritual practices. He was increasingly recognized as a leader in spirituality, morality, and in starting numerous social service projects. With each passing day, as more and more of his discourses spread among the masses, as more and more of the common people came to meet him, his true identity as a great moral leader of the world was becoming known.

Shrii Sarkar first spoke of Prout in 1959, and at that time formulated the five fundamental principles of Prout, which were later published in the final chapter of what is now his famous classic called *Idea and Ideology.* During the same time period, he toured extensively throughout India. By the year 1965 he took a long leave from his job and moved to Ananda Nagar, located in the spiritually vibrant heartland of Rahr in Purulia, West Bengal. Here, in one of the most impoverished regions of India, he began his mission - to work fulltime for the physical, mental and spiritual elevation of humanity.

Who was this propounder of the Prout economic model, which is panacea for the poor around the world, and whose principles he created only to alleviate the unbounded agonies, humiliations and sufferings of human beings everywhere? Some were beginning to whisper that Shrii Prabhat Ranjan Sarkar was a man of unprecedented love, compassion, magnanimity and uncompromising morality such as the world had never seen.

Shrii Sarkar was founder of the simple yet simultaneously vast and possibly complex paradigm called Prout, which stands for Progressive Utilization Theory. Its basic theme is progressive utilization and rational distribution of the earth's natural resources. It is not so complicated. The earth has plenty of resources to feed and nurture the entire human population of seven billion. And yet, a handful of greedy men hoard 90 percent of those resources for themselves alone. For this very reason, we have enormous human suffering pervading every corner of the earth.

Prout is the socio-economic-political side of Shrii Sarkar's total philosophy that mingles multiple concepts of spiritual, economic, political, social and cultural liberation. It is a critical aspect of his entire ideology, because in order to create a heaven on earth for the people of the earth, we need to first remove the great social ills besetting our planet. We also need to obliterate the existing economic paradigms which wreak havoc around the world with their hidden doctrines of intentionally increasing impoverization and ensuing massive suffering and starvation. Thus, Prout remains an absolute necessity to mitigate and then remove the sufferings of humanity and to pave the way for a golden dawn on earth.

However, as we all know, when anyone dares to speak the Absolute Truth in any sphere of life, the oppressors of humanity, the forces of darkness and immorality, greed and corruption, rush forward to suppress and silence that Truth. We also know that when a new idea is first propounded, it meets with tremendous resistance from the extant society, or rather from the forces controlling that society. From resistance emerges the next phase, when the idea's propounder faces intense persecution, and often torture and imprisonment. Thus, as the concepts of Prout and other aspects of his ideology spread and became popular among the masses, there were increasing attempts to suppress Prout by certain nefarious elements inside the Indian government as well as from the extant high caste elites, due to his uncompromising stance against ruthless economic exploitation, corruption, immorality, casteism, communalism and all other forms of political, social and economic injustice.

What was it that caused Prout to spread like wildfire in those days? What was it that caused hundreds, nay thousands, of people from all over India and the world to come and sit at his feet? It was his love. Even to read the words in his books, the words of his discourses, put one into an enthralled state, a state of intoxication. When reading those discourses, one felt that Shrii Sarkar was absolutely fearless, the lion of all lions. But also one felt, when reading those same discourses, how sweet he was. From his discourses emanated a flow of sweet charm that touched the heart and made people feel that yes, they could fight and overcome all exploitation in the society, and that yes, it was actually possible to completely transform the world.

In December, 1971, as persecution of Shrii Sarkar intensified, he was falsely accused of various crimes and imprisoned for nearly seven years. However, imprisonment could not break him. As one of the central jail officials said, "Even Napoleon was tamed by jail, but this living tiger cannot be tamed."

On February 12, 1973, he was seriously poisoned by an overdose of barbiturates administered by the prison doctor, after which he went on a protest fast, challenging the authorities who were not responding to his repeated calls for a critical inquiry into his poisoning. The poisoning left him in a weak and bedridden condition for the remaining five years of his imprisonment. Throughout this period he survived on a cup of salted whey twice a day.

History bears testimony that whenever a person states the absolute truth in any sphere of life, whether it be spiritual, social, economic or otherwise; sought clarification of doubts or protested against injustice and wrongs, the evil forces forthwith plotted against the person, administered poison, slandered and assaulted that person with rage, misused authority and mercilessly dealt blow after blow; but the blows boomeranged and ultimately the evil forces were annihilated by those very blows. Remember, by an unalterable decree of history, the evil forces are destined to meet their final doom.

Shrii Prabhat Ranjan Sarkar

Historical Echoes

Eight long years of his torture by the extant political authorities can take our memories back to the many great and illumined personalities in history who were tortured and even killed only due to their fight for justice, for their fight to simply tell the Absolute Truth to the people, for their unbounded determination to establish righteousness on earth.

For his revolutionary poetry and neohumanistic ideas, Kabir was endlessly persecuted. Sant Ravidas, who protested his entire life against the caste system, was finally murdered by Brahmins.

The great saint Tukaram was having a Jain book denouncing casteism translated into Marathi, and to block this work, he was also killed by Brahmin priests. Shri Chaitanya Mahaprabhu spread such profound love to millions that it was causing the unification of people from all castes and all walks of life. The jealousy of the priests became unbounded, and together the Brahmins and the Maharaja of Puri chopped him into little pieces and threw the pieces into the ocean. This unknown fact of history was revealed by Shrii Sarkar to his followers.

The great Egyptian scientist, mathematician and spiritual philosopher, Hypatia, was dragged from the street into a church and chopped into pieces by a mob of Christian fundamentalists because she preached against religious intolerance and because she was a woman who had great power in the society. The fundamentalists could not tolerate that a woman had so much moral power and respect in the society. Even today, fundamentalists everywhere cannot tolerate the moral rise of any woman. The man who ordered her death, Cyril of Alexandria, was later made a saint by the church.

The great French mystic Marguerite Porete was burned at the stake for having ideas that preached non-dualism. In addition, she spoke on a regular basis against the authority of priesthood. She founded the movement called "Free in Spirit", which was a movement to liberate the human spirit from all limitations, including the dogma of the church. The first scripture of this movement was written by Porete. In essence, she was the follower of advaita or non-dualism.

Poetic genius Guru Arjan fought relentlessly against communalism as he created unprecedented unity between Hindus and Muslims, and consequently the fundamentalists had him tortured until he died. Muslim fundamentalist, Sirhindi, who was responsible for his death, became an influential thinker and was one of the founders of Islamic fundamentalism in South Asia. Even today he is looked upon as a saint. Guru Tegh Bahadur was beheaded by Muslim fundamentalists only for trying to protect the rights of people of another religion from forcible conversion to Islam.

Sarmad, the Sufi poet from Armenia, was killed by Aurangzeb for going beyond all religions and spreading these ideas in his poetry. The Muslim guru of intense, selfless love, Mansur Al-Hallaj, was also murdered by Muslim fundamentalists for propagating absolute union with the Lord. The great Iranian mystic philosopher

Shahab al-Din Suhrawardi was killed by the son of Saladin, at the behest of Muslim fundamentalists, for fusing different religions and philosophies. He was trying to create a synthesis going beyond any one religion, and thus was going against Islamic dogma.

Hence, we should understand that the great personalities in any era of history face unbounded persecution as soon as they begin their fight for justice and dharma and for their courageous attempt to implement neohumanism. Was the founder of Prout any exception? No. For eight long years he was mercilessly tortured and humiliated in prison. Only a handful of persons know of those tortures today. Rather, these tremendous sacrifices made by Shrii Prabhat Ranjan Sarkar in prison have been almost entirely forgotten.

Prime Minister Indira Gandhi and her communist allies became obsessed with destroying Prout, due to the adamantine morality of its founder and his completely non-compromising stance on issues of justice and injustice. The prime concern of Shrii Sarkar was always the welfare of the common people. At the time of his arrest, a CBI official (obviously at the behest of the Government of India) offered him a ministerial berth in Indira Gandhi's cabinet if he issued a statement that, though he propounded Prout, he was not a Proutist. To which his characteristic reply was, "My dear gentleman! If ever I will be born as an animal, I will think over your august advice." In 1975 Indira Gandhi declared a state of emergency, banning Prout and arresting many of his followers – so great was her fear of the short, five foot three, bespectacled man clad in simple kurta and dhoti, who history will remember as Shrii Prabhat Ranjan Sarkar.

Throughout his stay in prison he condemned the corruption of jail officials and the government, despite its attempts to assassinate him. If the strategy behind his jailing had been to suppress and root out the Prout movement that Shrii Sarkar had spearheaded, this attempt by the Indian government failed miserably. During his incarceration, Shrii Sarkar's political and economic theories spread to more than 60 countries, and continued to spread at great speed. In 1977 an international organization called Proutist Universal was launched with its headquarters in Copenhagen. The aims of Proutist Universal are to propagate the ideals of Prout and to support social movements with similar ideals. By the mid-1980s Proutist Universal was established in practically all countries of the world.

In 1978 all charges against Shrii Sarkar were quashed, and he was released in August of that year to a tremendous welcome by thousands of his followers from all over the world. Throughout the remainder of his life, Shrii Sarkar continued to work tirelessly, twenty hours a day, for the suffering, downtrodden human beings and for the upliftment of all people. His contributions in the fields of science, philosophy, economics, agriculture and linguistics are so vast that it will take centuries before scholars can properly assess his real value to humanity.

Sarkar's cremation in 1990 in Kolkata, West Bengal was attended by thousands of followers from around the world. Yet still, his clarion call continues to ring in our ears.

Garda Ghista

With cosmic ideation, set out from the starting
point of moralism and advance towards supreme
realization. Your feet may bleed, cut by the thorns
scattered on the road. The sky, rent asunder by
the lightning and crashing thunder of the fearful
storm, may fall on your head; but proceed you
must. You are a born fighter. To flee the battle
in fear and hide like a corpse in the hills is
ultra vires to your existential vitality. You must
advance towards the Supreme Entity, your original
abode, smashing all obstacles on the path.

Shrii Prabhat Ranjan Sarkar

PROUT

The history of trade can be represented by four phases: (1) the mercantile division of labor, wherein surplus of goods was caused by geography, climate, and the availability of animals and plants. (2) the industrial division of labor, wherein machines began to replace people in the production of goods, causing more workers to be dependent on wages and leading to the first worker strikes; (3) the imperial division of labor, wherein companies moved to developing countries where workers sweated and scrounged to find raw materials for companies to ship back to their home countries; (4) the transnational era, wherein corporations take over entire national economies and directly control their resources.

Increasingly, production of goods has now shifted almost entirely to countries like India and China where wages come to mere pennies per worker per week. In addition, developing countries do not have the labor law restrictions of western countries, hence even ten-year-old children work in Chinese, Indian and Bangladeshi factories making goods for western export. Globalization has drastically reduced the power of national governments to take care of its citizens. Today corporations do indeed rule the world.

Concerned citizens everywhere, observing the effects of globalization over the past several decades, have begun grassroots movements in an effort to regain control of their local economies. The process of moving from the global to the local has been called localization. The force propelling this process is the desire for an economy that protects the people and rebuilds local communities. To be engaged in this process requires the courage to publicly reject the mantra of "international competitiveness" that is repeated worldwide by big business, financiers and mainstream economists, and replace it with new words such as "local sustainability", "cooperative economy" and "economic democracy". Concerned citizens engaged in the struggle to improve their local region no longer listen to the idea that every country must economically out-compete every other country. Instead of purchasing products from the cheapest source, which may be Brazil or China, it is more beneficial to the people if those same products are produced locally, even if the cost of production and hence the final price to the consumer is higher.

The Universal Declaration of Human Rights guarantees every human being the right to food, clothing, shelter, employment, education and health care, to justice, and especially the right to take part in the decisions that affect our lives. In a society dominated by corporations whose goal is maximum profit, human beings will not have these rights. Localization does not mean closing off the outside world. It means becoming more self-sufficient and less dependent on imports. When we gain control over our local economies, our lives will have more stability. Our jobs will be more stable.

What is local? Shrii Sarkar refers to the lowest socio-economic unit as a block, or an area comprising approximately 100,000 persons. In developing countries blocks will refer to reserved or abandoned lands, groups of villages or medium-sized towns. In a Prout economy, planning will take place at the central, state, district and block levels, with blocks being the smallest in size but in fact the engine for economic planning. Division into blocks is critical for bringing about economic decentralization.

As Shrii Sarkar has outlined, blocks will be formed based on very specific factors, such as physical features of the land, including river basins, climate, topography, flora and fauna and soil conditions, along with assessment of the socio-economic problems and needs of the people residing on that land. Problems that may arise requiring the cooperation of one or more blocks (including on both sides of international borders) can be dealt with by inter-block planning. Such problems may include soil erosion, flood control, drought and ensuing famine, reforestation, energy generation and communication systems, All higher level planning will be carried out by representatives from each block meeting at the district, then state and then central level. In future, central planning will further evolve into global planning.

This system of grassroots planning from block to district to region means that instead of individuals and communities being indifferent or feeling powerless, every individual will become involved in the economic future of the community. We need to each participate in the process of changing our economy from global to local.

Shrii Sarkar says that since the handful of capitalists presently controlling the global economy will never voluntarily give up their vast power, it is up to the common people to start a global movement in which the slogan should be: "Abolish centralized economy to end exploitation; establish decentralized economy!"

Shrii Sarkar has advocated that bartering take place as

much as possible as a means for acquiring essential goods and services. Venezuelan President Hugo Chavez has led the world in reviving the barter system by providing oil to other countries in exchange for goods and skills needed in Venezuela, such as doctors, medical skills and cows.

What are the primary tenets of Prout that prove themselves so threatening to the extant forces in power? Among the more important tenets of Prout are Shrii Sarkar's principles of economic decentralization and requirements for economic democracy. They are important because, if implemented, they will sound the death knell for capitalism which presently wreaks economic havoc and destruction around the earth, as it allows for human greed to grow undisturbed and unhampered. The greed of one man leads to the suffering of thousands or millions of others. For this very reason we can say that the capitalist economic model is an inhuman model. It is high time that the world shift to a new paradigm which will provide economic, political, moral, cultural and spiritual succour to the entire world citizenry. Shrii Sarkar once said, "Don't you know why I propounded Prout? When such atrocities are being done to the living beings who are verily the divinity in disguise, then do you think I, as Guru, can sit still and watch? It is my duty to help them."

Prout is a decentralized economic model with cooperatives as its bedrock. In the words of Shrii Sarkar, "Economic planning must start from the lowest level, from the grassroots, where the knowledge, experience and talent of local people can be applied to solve local problems and build local economies." The goal of world trade must be to protect the local people, not politicians or owners of corporations. The "local" in localization can refer to a nation state or, as in the case of larger nations like the U.S., Canada or Russia, it can refer to a particular bioregion, state or province within the larger nation. It means simply to bring economic control back to the local arena. Localization does not refer to "state" control, as in the communist model. It refers to local people in a town. Every person must have a voice and a vote in the economic direction of their community.

Shrii Sarkar advocates an economic structure wherein the production and distribution of each product is assigned either to the public, cooperative or private sector. In other words, there would be some businesses too small or too complex to function as cooperatives and hence should be run as small, private enterprises. Similarly, other businesses would be too large to be cooperatively managed (i.e., energy, communications) and would then be managed as regional public utilities. However, all other businesses would follow the cooperative business model. In particular, as per Prout, the essential necessities of life will never be in the hands of private enterprise.

While the bedrock of PROUT is shifting businesses from the corporate to the cooperative model, other strategies are required to attain and maintain economic decentralization and to assist in moving communities towards economic democracy. For example, Shrii Sarkar advocates that all resources in a socio-economic region be controlled by local people. This particularly applies to those resources essential in providing the minimum necessities of life – food, water, clothing, housing, health care and education. We should think in terms of production being based on consumption and not on profit. All goods produced in a community or bioregion would also be sold in that community. This will keep local money continually rolling inside the community, resulting in both income as well as purchasing power continually increasing. It will also lead to job stability. In a centralized economy, this simply does not happen except for a minority of people. To further hasten decentralization, production and distribution of goods must be carried out directly by cooperatives without middlemen.

An additional strategy would be that only local people are to be employed in local business enterprises. This alone will solve the problem of unemployment. Furthermore, no outside interference should be allowed in a local economy. Still another idea propagated by Shrii Sarkar that we need to consider is that all essential goods not produced locally should as far as possible be removed from local stores. It is a radical concept in the present era of globalization. However, taking such a step would compel local communities to become self-sufficient. Also we can remember that the shorter the distance between producer and consumer, the greater control of the economy by the consumer. If less essential or non-essential items are imported into a region, it will not be so harmful.

With imminent water crises on every continent of the earth and hence coming food shortages, people must think now in terms of moving towards local production of all essential food and non-food items as soon as possible. Once products essential for existence are produced locally, then people can bring in less essential and non-essential (luxury) items. It is expected that this would be a gradual process and can only be achieved with education; i.e., when people realize that it is in the best interest of their community to grow local, produce local, sell local and buy local. This process of localization, of community struggle for sovereignty over their local economy, is the seed for the establishment of economic democracy, which is the very essence of Prout.

Money helps one attain temporary liberation
from afflictions, but that money is also limited.
If someone accumulates money, another person
is deprived of it; so no one should accumulate an
unlimited amount. Some means must be discovered
to remove human afflictions. With this in mind
I have formulated a new socio-economic theory
which will remove those afflictions. It is called
PROUT. PROUT alone can save humanity from its
woes. It is useless to preach the gospels of spiritual
salvation to a person who has no food to eat.

Shrii Prabhat Ranjan Sarkar

Cooperatives the Bedrock of Prout

While the principles mentioned earlier for establishing decentralized economies are clear guidelines, the overriding factor in decentralized economies will be cooperatives. The goal is to move from a capitalist economy to a cooperative commonwealth. American universities, in their macro and micro economics courses, teach three types of business models: (1) proprietorship, i.e., single owner, (2) partnership, i.e., two or more owners of a company, and (3) corporation, which has multiple shareholders. However, the fourth business model, which is the cooperative business model, is omitted entirely from ninety-nine percent of American economics courses.

We can give the example of any Walmart outlet where a minimum of twenty women are employed, earning minimum wage and barely making ends meet. If those twenty women were to form a cooperative of any kind - a health food store, a corner mini-mart, or a dairy cooperative, raising cows and selling the fresh milk, later expanding to make fresh butter and cheese - they will work for living wages, and they will get their equal and fair share of surplus funds at the end of each year. They will no longer be slaves to a wealthy man. In the cooperative, the women are both employees and owners.

All share in the work and all share in the surplus. Together the women decide how much surplus is ploughed back into the business and how much goes to the owners/ employees as annual dividends. This business model can help all women to escape poverty.

Cooperatives lead to humane, democratic production. Wages must be kept as close together as possible to avoid the entry of classism. Tasks should be divided as equally as possible. Other precautions are necessary, such as taking care that the collectively appointed manager of the cooperative does not misuse his position to take excessive control of its management.

In 1844 the weavers of Rochdale, England formed a cooperative and wrote up the "Principles of Cooperation." These principles later became the "Principles of the International Cooperative Alliance." They continue to form the bedrock of cooperatives around the world, and are as follows:

Principle 1: Voluntary and Open Membership.

Cooperatives are voluntary organizations, open to all persons able to use their services and willing to accept the responsibilities of membership, without gender, social, racial, political or religious discrimination.

Principle 2: Democratic Member Control.

Cooperatives are democratic organizations controlled by their members, who actively participate in setting policies and making decisions. Men and women serving as elected representatives are accountable to the membership. In primary cooperatives members have equal voting rights (one member, one vote) and cooperatives at other levels are also organized in a democratic manner.

Principle 3: Member Economic Participation.
Members contribute equitably to, and democratically control, the capital of their cooperative. At least part of that capital is usually the common property of the cooperative. Members generally receive limited compensation, if any, on capital subscribed as a condition of membership. Members allocate surpluses for any or all of the following purposes: developing their cooperative, possibly by setting up reserves, part of which at least would be indivisible; benefiting members in proportion to their transactions with the cooperative; and supporting other activities approved by the membership.

Principle 4: Autonomy and Independence.
Cooperatives are autonomous, self-help organizations controlled by their members. If they enter into agreements with other organizations, including governments, or raise capital from external sources, they do so on terms that ensure democratic control by their members and maintain their cooperative autonomy.

Principle 5: Education, Training and Information.
Cooperatives provide education and training for their members, elected representatives, managers, and employees so they can contribute effectively to the development of their cooperatives. They inform the general public, particularly young people and opinion leaders. regarding the nature and benefits of those cooperatives.

Principle 6: Cooperation among Cooperatives.
Cooperatives serve their members most effectively and strengthen the cooperative movement by working together through local, regional, national and international structures.

Principle 7: Concern for Community.
Cooperatives work for the sustainable development of their communities through policies approved by their members.

All cooperative organizations, in order to best serve the interests of their members and communities, should actively cooperate in every practical way with other cooperatives at local, national and international levels. The idea is to establish a global network of cooperative economies

The quest for profits and privilege in a society leads to unending crime, corruption, immorality, poverty and wars. The only solution is to introduce the cooperative business model at every level, for all production and distribution, and for administration of economic issues. Cooperatives can bring about real economic democracy, which in turn can foster genuine political democracy. The critical factor to remove is the profit motive, due to its de-humanizing influence on human beings. It must be replaced by the far more humane mindset of thinking for collective welfare above individual welfare. This change of mindset is an evolutionary process that more and more people will accept as they witness the great benefits from working in cooperatives.

Shrii Sarkar also says that changing to the cooperative model will be a gradual and voluntary process. It cannot be forced upon the people. People need to be educated and convinced regarding its benefits. At present the poverty may not be severe enough for people to consider the cooperative option. However, many states of India have unemployment levels surpassing forty percent. In Detroit, USA, the unemployment rate is also more than forty percent. This economic tragedy will serve to propel the common people to look for alternative solutions and thus the suffering humanity will gravitate towards the cooperative paradigm and way of life.

Shrii Sarkar divides the cooperative sector into four branches: (1) farmer cooperatives, (2) producer cooperatives, (3) consumer cooperatives and (4) service cooperatives. The chief advantage of the agricultural cooperative system is that farmers do not need to sell their produce immediately as they do in the private enterprise or capitalist system. The cooperative can advance money to the farmers so that they can sustain themselves while waiting for the most opportune time to sell their crops, keeping enough produce aside to last their families for one year. Cooperatives can directly fix the prices and bypass the middlemen entirely. Thus the cooperative structure will serve to protect and shelter the farmers financially.

Farmer cooperatives can in turn sell their produce directly to producer cooperatives, which utilize those raw materials for manufacturing all sorts of consumer products. Producer cooperatives will include agro-industries, agrico-industries and non-agricultural industries. Industrial cooperatives include large-scale factories which should be primarily assembly factories. Both small-scale and large-scale industrial cooperatives should be created.

Aside from creating an entirely new moral culture based on collective, selfless, benevolent thinking, the greatest economic advantage of cooperatives is that in such an economy, the question of unemployment will not arise. Unemployment only occurs in the capitalist framework where the goal is profit instead of consumption. If any unemployment arises in a cooperative-based community, it will be solved by substantial reduction in work hours for all members of the community without reduction in income or purchasing power.

Consumer cooperatives will distribute all kinds of consumer goods to the public. Some products will come in the category of essential goods, others as demi-essential, i.e., survival is possible without these items, and others as non-essential, i.e., luxury items. Consumer cooperatives can be formed by people who share the surplus as per their individual labor contribution and capital investment. If they take on the role of manager they can also receive a salary from the cooperative. Consumer cooperatives will purchase goods directly from producer and agricultural cooperatives so as to block the possibility of hoarding by individual traders or middlemen.

One more category of cooperatives is service cooperatives, which will come within the sphere of cultural cooperatives. Doctors, for example, can start a cooperative together. This will also solve any unemployment problem in the medical profession.

In time we can establish banking cooperatives, housing cooperatives and funeral cooperatives. The very structure of the cooperative in all these cases will lead to benevolence of mind and thinking first for the collective and second for oneself.

What would a cooperative commonwealth look like? What would it feel like? When we establish such a commonwealth, we will see thousands of citizens living in their own cooperative houses, supplied by their own stores, working in their own cooperative agricultural and other industries, which are financed by their own cooperative banks. We will see the people entertaining themselves in their own cooperatively-owned playgrounds, and their cooperative children's homes and homes for the elderly and disabled. All will be taken care of under the cooperative system. What we will be witnessing is a veritable utopian society, which theorists and dreamers long for but have no vision of how to implement in real life.

Shifting from the proprietor and corporate business models to a cooperative commonwealth will not occur in a day. It cannot work unless the common people are wholly convinced that the new financial structure will bring concrete benefits. It will involve constant and extensive education along with practical demonstration. Just see what Shrii Sarkar has to say about the cooperative model: "The sweetest unifying factors are love and sympathy for humanity. The wonts of the human heart are joy, pleasure and beatitude. In the physical realm the best expression of this human sweetness is the cooperative system. The cooperative system is the best representation of the sweet nectar of humanity." When expressed with such deep adoration for humanity, then is it possible to resist these tender words? Are we not then duty bound to manifest his dream for a cooperative commonwealth at the earliest?

According to PROUT, in the first phase of agrarian revolution, private ownership of land within the cooperative system will be recognized. People should have the right to employ labour for cultivation, but in such cases fifty percent of the total produce should be distributed as wages to the agricultural labourers who work in the cooperative. That is, the owners of the land will get fifty percent of the total produce and those who create the produce through their labour will get the other fifty percent. This ratio must never decrease – rather it should increase in favour of the agricultural labourers who work in the cooperative. The managerial staff body of the cooperative should only be constituted from among those who have shares in the cooperative. They will be elected. Their positions should not be honorary because that creates scope for corruption.

Shrii Prabhat Ranjan Sarkar

Economic Decentralization
the Key

Shrii Sarkar provides the following five principles for creating and maintaining a decentralized economy:

(1) All resources in a socio-economic unit should be controlled by the local people. This applies particularly to those resources that are essential in providing the minimum necessities of life. Raw materials should be converted by the local people into finished products to be sold locally. Shrii Sarkar defines "local people" as those who have merged their individual socio-economic interests with the interests of the local, socio-economic unit. Hence, the term "local people" has no relation to one's race, complexion, language or birthplace. The one point of consideration is whether an individual has made that geographical region and community as his own, and whether he has merged his individual socio-economic interests with the collective. If an individual has not done this, then he would not be deemed as a local person, and hence would have no say as regards local socio-economic issues, for example, as regards production and distribution of either natural resources or their finished products. Surplus wealth, after meeting the needs of the local people, can be distributed to those having greater merit, such as doctors, engineers, scientists and teachers. These

persons with highly specialized knowledge and acumen can be provided with extra amenities that will help them in their profession. However, the goal of the community will be to constantly reduce the economic gap between the wealthiest person and the poorest person.

(2) Shrii Sarkar's second principle for maintaining a successful decentralized economy, as emphasized earlier, is that production must be based on consumption and not on profit. In a decentralized economy, all goods produced will be sold in the local community. Hence, a sound economic and equitable structure will be established. This practice will also cause the local money to be continually flowing inside the community, which will further strengthen the economy and make it practically immune from any upheaval or depression. With the constant internal circulation of money, both incomes as well as people's purchasing capacity will go on increasing. This has never been achieved with the communist model or the capitalist model.

(3) The third principle for maintaining a healthy, decentralized economy is that production and distribution of all natural resources and finished products must be carried out by cooperatives. It is extremely difficult for cooperatives to survive when surrounded by capitalist enterprises. The prices of goods sold by cooperatives cannot compete with the prices of Walmart corporation, which has their goods made in China often by ten-year-old children earning a few pennies a day, then has those goods flown directly to private air terminals next to Walmart headquarters. The consequences of Walmart's actions are that (1) local people who could have produced those goods are without jobs and hence do not even have money to shop at Walmart; (2) small children and women in China

are paid pittance and work 70-80 hours per week making those products; (3) people employed in Walmart stores earn pittance and receive no benefits. Hence, Walmart engages in a full, global circle of exploitation to end up ranked as one of the top ten richest companies in the world.

According to Shrii Sarkar's first principle, Walmart does not classify as a "local" person. Hence, it must be removed from the community and replaced by local companies managed by local people to produce many of the same goods produced by slave labor in China for Walmart. The final price of locally made goods will be higher; however, people will not mind those slightly higher prices with the realization that local people are gainfully employed in producing and selling those goods and are receiving living wages for their work. Living wages and adequate purchasing power will be guaranteed because the business model of all companies created in communities will be the cooperative business model. Raw materials, i.e., the natural resources of a bioregion, will provide constant supplies to cooperative businesses that can produce finished goods and sell them in the local market. When people of a community understand the benefits of the cooperative business model, they will accept it whole-heartedly. Agriculture, industry and trade can all be organized through cooperatives. Private ownership of these industries can be abolished because in private ownership the well-being of the larger community will not be served. Cooperatives and decentralization are inseparable.

(4) The fourth principle required of a decentralized economy is that local people must be employed in local business enterprises. If they are not employed in local

businesses, the problem of unemployment cannot be solved. Local people should collectively decide on the minimum requirements essential for their physical and economic well-being. It is critical that no outside interference is allowed in a local economy. People knowledgeable in agriculture, in agro-industries (industries related to farm production) as well as agrico-industries (industries related to products from farming, i.e., silk from sericulture, rope from jute) will be able to work in agricultural cooperatives.

(5) The fifth and perhaps the most difficult principle to implement is that all goods not produced locally should be removed from local stores. The goal of decentralization is for communities to become self-sufficient. So long as imported goods are available, there will be no incentive for blocks and regions to produce those goods. So long as imported goods are available, the people will not be guaranteed employment in local cooperative industries. For this reason, banishing all imported products is critical to a community in the process of becoming economically empowered. Local products may not be as cheap as imported goods. They also may not be as efficient or technically sophisticated. Nevertheless, this principle is essential in order to create self-sustaining communities. During times of economic collapse, as we saw in the 1930s, it is only self-sufficient communities that will be able to survive and reasonably cope during hard times. Self-sustaining communities will be immune to inflation and deflation. Bringing in imported products means the money gained in sales of those products will not remain in the community. It will leave and travel to the company owner who may be in another state or even another country. Money leaving a community will cause it to suffer. In order for people to prosper, money must

remain in a town and must keep circulating through production, sales and continually improving production and increasing wages.

If any item can be produced locally, it should not be imported. Several centuries ago, when men ventured by ship to India for spices and other luxuries, they brought products back to their home countries that were unavailable locally. This motto must be revived. Global trade must be used only to acquire essential items that cannot be produced locally. It is the premise of the "fair trade" movement. This will protect local jobs and cooperative businesses. If goods are produced and sold locally, money returns to the producing cooperative, and profits are given to the employee-owners in the form of dividends. All money involved in production and sales remains in the area. This money can be used to create more cooperatives or to strengthen the economic infrastructure. Resource and other taxes can be introduced to help cover the costs of converting from a global to a local economy. Thus only that trade should be undertaken that enhances and strengthens local economies and environments. The shorter the distance between producer and consumer, the greater the control of that economy by the consumers.

While it may be difficult to establish village-level economic infrastructure at present, there is no insurmountable obstacle preventing us from establishing block-level economic infrastructure. As far as possible, the establishment, operation and distribution of all industries should be done at the block level. Only when this cannot be done should industries be organized at a higher level. Obviously, industries such as iron and steel factories cannot function in every village, block and district, so they should function in a larger area. There are some special types of key industries which can conveniently function as either small-scale industries or medium-scale cooperative industries. If some key industries are structured in this way, they must be under state control. Care should be taken to ensure that they are properly organized and widespread. Such key industries should never be controlled by capitalists, otherwise the interests of the people will be partially if not fully ignored...Normally only very large-scale key industries should be under state control, and these industries should be centralized instead of decentralized. But industries which cannot be readily decentralized today may be decentralized in the future due to changing circumstances. At that time the decentralization of key industries must be implemented.

Shrii Prabhat Ranjan Sarkar

Prout - Panacea for the Poor

Why are we saying that Prout is the panacea for the poor? Shrii Sarkar has provided four simple requirements for the implementation of economic democracy, as follows: (1) The minimum requirements of a particular age – water, food, clothing, housing, education and health care - must be guaranteed to all citizens; (2) Increasing purchasing capacity must be guaranteed to all citizens. In fact, adequate purchasing capacity of every person must be guaranteed in the national constitution; (3) The power of making economic decisions must lie entirely with the local people; and (4) Outsiders, non-local people, must in no way be allowed to interfere in local economies. This will stop the outflow of capital, the present cause of impoverization. These four requirements if implemented, along with the principles necessary to create a decentralized economy, will lead people closer to economic democracy, because the power to control the economy will lie with the people. When outside ownership of local land and resources is prohibited, and when lands and resources are owned collectively by the people who live on those lands, at that point in time poverty will cease to exist, and will become a relic in the history museum. Is this not a glorious dream to envision?

Shrii Sarkar states that thirty-five percent of the workforce should be in agriculture. In the United States the myth that there are too many farmers, when in fact only two percent of the workforce is in agriculture, has caused the migration of millions of people in rural areas to the towns and cities. Farmers in America have been replaced to a large extent by machinery, chemicals, fuel and credit on factory farms. Even at two percent, more farmers continue to file for bankruptcy and move in desperation to the cities looking for work. Many never find work and come under the category of the permanently unemployable.

We see here two serious societal issues that should be solved urgently: (1) The propaganda by the US government to the common people not to farm should be reversed, until 30-35 percent of the population are engaged in agriculture, as per the guideline of Shrii Sarkar. (2) Every village, town and city in every country must immediately create a Department of Employment, and that department must be mandated to find jobs for all unemployed people, which is also a mandate of Shrii Sarkar. This should not be difficult to do, as always jobs will be available in the area of public works. Always there can be improvements to existing structures and institutions, and always there can be expansion in every arena of life.

When it comes to creating sustainable communities, one of the most urgent crises today is water. We need to bring water back to the earth. Shrii Sarkar has stated: "If it does not rain anywhere on earth for only one year, all life on the planet will be destroyed. This is because all creatures – from the smallest organisms to the largest animals – need water. If there is no water, first the small creatures will die, then the ecological balance of the planet will be lost. Next, human beings will also die, and soon the earth will become a barren wasteland." The prime known cause of drought is deforestation, the wanton destruction of plants and trees. With deforestation there are no longer plants which can nurture the soil. In forests the trees will keep both soil and water amidst its roots. For example, during the dry season in Bengal, one will see water trickling down near the fields. That water has been released from the roots of the standing crops. Once the crops are harvested, the water dries up. The problem of deforestation has been caused by human beings and can easily be solved by human beings

Here also Shrii Sarkar has provided us with detailed guidelines in the field of water conservation. The fastest way to increase water supplies is afforestation. We need to double the present quantity of surface water, something that can easily be done when there is a decentralized approach to water management. The depth of ponds and lakes should be increased.

The second step is to expand afforestation programs around all water bodies. This process can be multiplied by constructing new ponds and lakes and creating lakeside plantations. Lakeside and riverside plantations will stop soil erosion, nurture the top soil and provide a steady supply of water year round. According to Shrii Sarkar, five plant types should be planted around lakes: slope plants, boundary plants, wire plants, aquatic plants and surface plants. Slope plants include pineapple, asparagus, aloe vera, brinjal (eggplant) and chilli. These five hold the water in their roots and halt soil erosion. Slope plants should be planted in symmetrical horizontal rows and never in vertical lines, as in this case the water will flow away and lead to soil erosion. Terraces will help to prevent surface water runoff and check soil erosion. In general, all sloping land should be terraced. Mounds and furrows on slopes should be dug perpendicular to the slope.

Shrii Sarkar has provided us with boundless agricultural, horticultural and aquatic guidelines. He tells us further that boundary plants include palm trees and flower creepers, vegetables and fruits and that palm trees should be planted around lakes. This includes palm trees, coconut trees, Palmyra, betel nut palms, date palms and banana trees. Creepers can be grown together with the trees; specifically, black pepper creepers can be planted together with coconut trees, jasmine creepers with Palmyra trees, and medicinal creepers can be planted with date palms. Brick walls should be planted around the lake with wires running along the top. Plants should be grown along the wires. This includes creeping vegetables such as beans, bottle gourd, pumpkin, morning glory, moonflowers, melon, passion fruit and grapes. Aquatic plants can be planted in the water and include lotus, *Victoria regina*, water lilies and water chestnut. Using these strategies, water can be nurtured, stored and conserved year round. Water tables can be raised to just six meters below the ground or even higher. This is the goal. Hence, aside from check dams, watersheds and drip irrigation, it becomes essential, when planning for water conservation and checking of soil erosion, to create both river and lakeside plantations.

The same principles can be followed for developing riverside plantations, which will serve the same purpose as lakeside plantations, i.e., water conservation and flood prevention, regulation of water flow in the river and soil nourishment. Banyan tree, date palms, neem (margosa) tree, tamarind and fruit trees should all be planted along rivers. If horticulture is planted along riverbanks, the rivers will never be without water. Aside from horticulture, Shrii Sarkar advocates that tea gardens can also be grown along riverbanks. It is an excellent way to solve the problem of water shortage in northern Bengal.

In temperate climates forest gardens can be created along similar lines. By observing principles we can learn from the forests, we can plant edible layers of perennials that would provide either food, fuel or medicines, and in addition support the wildlife. By planting trees, shrubs, and perennial ground cover and vines, we can create what amounts to a sustainable food, fuel and medicine bank. We can create seven layers in our forest gardens, comprising roots, ground cover, herbs, fruiting shrubs, dwarf trees, tree canopy and finally tall trees, all of which can co-exist together in ecological equipoise. Vines can be planted to cover walls and fences along the border. We can also plant edible hedges specifically to attract bees and butterflies to the forest garden. Roses can be mixed with rhubarb and beetroot. Figs and quinces can be mixed in with native trees such as beech, oak and holly. Plants and trees that require heavy watering are to be avoided.

According to Shrii Sarkar, certain plants, such as *Albizzia lebbeck benth*, *Dalbergia sissoo Roxb*, the Himalayan white oak, i.e., *Quercus incana Roxb*, and ferns have the capacity to attract rain clouds. This fact should be widely propagated so that those particular plants can be grown in all arid and semi-arid regions of the world. This is also the kind of education that should be taught to villagers so as to help them to become self-reliant.

According to Shrii Sarkar, subterranean water should not be used for irrigation, as its use will cause the water table to fall, leading to acute water shortage. Rather, everything possible should be done to create more wetlands, which will raise the water table. The best system, hence, is to collect the surface water and the rainwater. All rainwater, even from drizzles or light showers, should be caught at the site and stored for later use. We know that in Libya the great man-made river of huge pipes has been constructed by taking water from the large aquifer under the desert in southeast Libya up to the coastal area full of human habitation. As a consequence, all water holes in the vicinity of the aquifer have dried up. Shrii Sarkar says that more harm than good may result in the emptying of underground aquifers. The solution then is to study all ways of catching rainwater and conserving the surface water, creating more and more wetlands.

Shrii Sarkar also informs us that constructing deep tube wells is not the answer to drought, even in desert conditions. Tube well irrigation causes the water table to drop. In some parts of the United Arab Emirates, for example, the water table is 1,000 feet below the earth, which is an untenable situation. However, the Bedouin do not know of other solutions. The water table is low there despite the fact that they are careful to conserve water on their farms in the desert and use only the drip irrigation system. Even the date trees are irrigated with drip irrigation.

The water table in any community should remain above 20-25 feet, as in this case surface vegetation will not suffer. If the water table drops below even 50 feet, however, the surface of the land will dry up and gradually turn into a desert within 50 years. If there is one deep tube well from which water is regularly drawn, it causes neighbouring shallow tube wells to dry up, leaving neighbours without drinking water.

In certain deep tube wells harmful elements such

as heavy minerals and mineral salts mix with the water, causing salinity. In this instance the land irrigated with such water will become unfit for farming. Deep tube wells can be used on a temporary basis only until more sustainable water conservation methods can be built which have no deleterious effects on the surrounding environment. These include river and reservoir irrigation, small check dams, ponds, canals, lakes, shift and lift irrigation. We need to always remember that when starting any sustainable community, the first order of work is the water supply and creating all kinds of water conservation projects, including wetlands.

If all the above guidelines of Shrii Sarkar are followed, humans will have ample surface water for their use and will not need to tap the subterranean water. While millions of trees need to be planted in every village, we can also create a very careful compendium of forest gardens containing all perennial plants which serve as food, fuel or as vital minerals for the roots of other plants. No one can say that the water crisis is unavoidable. It is indeed man-made but can be completely reversed with afforestation. Shrii Sarkar says clearly: "We must not forget even for a moment that the seed of destruction of the human race lies in the wanton destruction of forests. No more deforestation should be allowed. Our aim should be large-scale afforestation."

Shrii Sarkar provides concrete, constructive information in his discourses on farming, agriculture, horticulture, afforestation and many other topics. For example, he tells us that the stems of the okra can be used to cause pineapple trees to produce fruits and flowers. If the stems of the okra are burnt and scattered in the field of pineapple trees, the fumes and smoke will rise up and help the pineapple to produce fruit and flowers simultaneously.

Shrii Sarkar provides detailed information on inter-cropping or mixed cropping. As an example, he says, if the land is extremely rocky and there is no soil, then soil should be brought from elsewhere so that palm trees and custard apple (sitafel) saplings can be planted in between mulberry plants. If the soil is of somewhat better quality, then date palm and again custard apple can be planted between the mulberry plants.

Shrii Sarkar discusses lac culture or lacquer produced by insects grown on trees. In apiculture bees can produce honey and pure beeswax from many flowers. This would include wild bees such as the wild rock bees and bush bees, which can be domesticated. All bees should be welcome in community gardens. Bee boxes can be placed near oil seeds, flower gardens, neem (margosa) trees, Indian olive trees and grape plants.

We can venture to say that if all of Shrii Sarkar's ideas for sustainable development are implemented, then that community would experience ecological equilibrium, due to the deep respect for nature that is integral to the neohumanistic philosophy of Shrii Sarkar, as well as economic equipoise, due to the vast number of products suggested by him that can be made from the various plants. When we take Shrii Sarkar's principles of economic decentralization, his requirements for economic democracy, and his vast knowledge passed on to us relating to agriculture and potential agricultural products as well as sustainable farming methods, we are to understand that all these comprise the various aspects of a Prout economy. All these multifarious steps are required for the practical implementation of Prout. All these aspects must be studied by us so as to gain the big picture of what our Prout communities will look like. The urgent goal, then, is creation of these Prout sustainable communities following all economic, agricultural and other guidelines laid down by Shrii Sarkar.

As the Great Depression of the 21st century begins to take hold of the world, we can expect many things. Accelerated unemployment already stares us in the face, in every country. Mortgage foreclosures are skyrocketing, particularly in the source country of this Depression, which is the United States. We see credit card defaults, corporate and personal bankruptcy, poverty, unmanageable debt, domestic violence, child abuse, increased alcoholism and drug abuse, crime, homelessness, prostitution, divorce, abortions, child abandonment, gambling, suicide, sexually transmitted diseases, malnutrition, spiralling mental illness, excessive demand on charities for food and shelter, and finally a growing disregard for authority due to the rage and discontent brought on by the utter helplessness of poverty.

To add insult to extreme poverty, we will see accelerated inflation, such that even the basic essentials, including food, water, clothes, heating oil, electricity, phone and internet connection will become out of reach for millions. If this scenario lasts for an extended period, there is a real chance of civil unrest and resulting imposition of martial law. All these point to the absolute urgency of returning to an ecological lifestyle, if necessary moving to rural areas and learning new ways of becoming self-sufficient. It points to the absolute necessity of creating sustainable communities where people will control their own currency, their own agriculture, their own education, and can even get off the corporate electrical grid and produce their own energy, so that in no sphere will the common people be dependent on private corporations and governments for their survival.

In a Prout sustainable community, self-reliance is the key in farming. Farming should not be dependent on outside resources. Rather, Shrii Sarkar says it should be integrated with all aspects, such as "agriculture, horticulture, floriculture, sericulture, silk culture, apiculture, dairy farming, animal husbandry, irrigation, pisciculture, pest control, using organic fertilizers, cottage industries, energy production, research centers and water conservation."

Also, in a Prout-based sustainable community, animals will never be slaughtered, nor will they be sold for slaughter. Instead, prosperous dairy farming can be done having milk production from dairy cows, goats, sheep and buffaloes. Milk powder and dehydrated yogurt can be produced and sold after giving to all the community residents. In a PROUT community all animals are to be loved and nurtured as per Shrii Sarkar's philosophy of Neohumanism which propagates the concept of universalism, i.e., loving and respecting not just other human beings but all creatures and even the inanimate objects.

The distinguishing feature between ecologists and economists is the factor of ethics or justice. When we bring ethics into economics, then it is no longer about cost-benefit analysis. It becomes an issue of whether any action taken will harm anything: will it harm humans, or will it harm the animals and plants? The entire ecosystem is taken into consideration.

Not only is this a problem of economics versus ecology, it is a problem of a highly exploitative, profit-driven economic model called capitalism. In capitalism only profit is considered. Externalities and spill-over effects are irrelevant to a capitalist. Capitalists are represented herein as the owners and CEOs of agri-corporations who do not hesitate to lay waste to a region via chemical pollution or exhausting its water supplies in the name of corporate profit. So the issue is not only one of moving from economics to ecology, or ecological economics. It is also an issue of moving from an immoral, inhumane economic system to a kinder, gentler and sweeter economic paradigm that has morality at its core. The morality stems from putting human, animal and plant life at the very top of the pyramid, and putting other issues further down the pyramid. The morality of Prout is rooted in an internal oath taken by every moralist to never harm another living creature.

Shrii Sarkar has stated that the sufferings of the people are the direct result of the sins of the leaders. In view of World Bank statistics indicating that governments did not change poverty/wealth ratios or alleviate the economic suffering of the people, the question arises: do we have any choice regarding adoption of the PROUT economic model? If, for example, communities switch to the cooperative business model and begin producing their own essential commodities, then domestic or global monetary collapse will either not affect or will only minimally affect those communities. They can even develop their own currencies and utilize the barter system as much as possible - another key feature of Prout.

In the words of Shrii Sarkar, "Human movement is movement towards ecological equipoise – towards the supreme synthesis. In the inner world, balance must be maintained as this leads to spiritual progress. Ecological order is not only for the earth but for the entire universe, and it must be maintained both within and without... balance must be maintained between the internal and external spheres. In all aspects of human life this subtle balance must be maintained. This is ecological equipoise."

As we search for sustainable development bereft of ecological destruction, we should acknowledge that the new, ecologically sound societies originated in the Third World and will be regained there also. In other words, it is the Third World people who will lead the way towards planetary ecological equilibrium. We need to hearken back to traditional, indigenous, agricultural practices and give renewed importance to agriculture as the bedrock of our lives. It will be the first step in a continuing process of development, which will include adopting ecologically secure policies to meet everyone's basic necessities in the areas of water, food, clothing, shelter, health care, education and information. We can collectively decide which products are essential, useful and safe for human adaptation, always bearing in mind that the entire planet of people must be taken care of in an equitable manner. As Shrii Sarkar reminds us, no one is to be left behind.

An ideal sustainable community will incorporate even more than the above. It will incorporate not just ecological and economic equilibrium. If we can create a moral revolution in our own community, then there is nothing stopping us from expanding that to a global moral revolution. From every standpoint – political, economic, social, cultural, moral and spiritual – we need a total transformation. In fact this was the life mission of Shrii Sarkar. The ideal community should not merely be physically sustainable, it should be sustainable in every other aspect of life as well. Hence, the work of building such a community is never-ending. We need to create bioregional, self-sufficient communities that by definition will be protected from future economic as well as ecological and climatic calamities.

There are several common points which should be implemented in all master units [Prout sustainable communities]: schools, hostels, children's homes, medical units, cottage industries, dairy farms, plantations, flour mills, bakeries, seed banks, cheap seed distribution centers, free plant distribution centers, biogas plants, apiculture, butter production, and ideal farm training centres... Our [Prout sustainable communities] should undertake schemes to construct houses for extremely poor people. This special housing scheme for the poor must be immediately established. Our [sustainable community] program is a combination of oriental sublimity and western dynamicity.

Shrii Prabhat Ranjan Sarkar

From Resistance to Revolution to Peace

As Sarkar has stated, capitalism turns men into beggars and communism turns beggars into beasts. The world today is controlled by oligopolies - a few companies, controlled by a handful of extremely wealthy men, that sell goods to other people or companies. The food industry has likewise become an oligopoly. For example, the banana market is dominated by an oligopoly of five companies. These mega corporations squeeze the farmers and pit one country's farmers against another country's. The farmers do the only thing they can do, which is to squeeze and cut labor costs.

Oligopolies (a handful of sellers) invariably lead to oligopsonies (a handful of buyers). The supermarket industry is a further example of an oligopsony, where just three major supermarket chains exist in the US: Safeway, Kroger and Albertson's. These three have bought out most smaller chains, a step that gives them tremendous power, leading to oligopsony exploitation, which has led to severely reduced income for farmers as the oligopsony of produce buyers squeezes prices, using their power to select the lowest price from amongst the helpless farmers. In addition, growers in the United States, for example, are expected to not only sell at a cheaper price but are obliged by the buyer oligopoly to market and promote their produce inside the supermarkets. In the produce sphere, supermarket chains are now an oligonomy, which means they are both the buyers (oligopoly) and the sellers (oligopsony). The supermarkets are the middlemen and use their "middle" position to exploit in either direction. It is interesting to note here that Venezuelan President Hugo Chavez eliminates middlemen in every sphere of the economy, both in Venezuela as well as in his program to supply oil to poor Americans, Cubans and people of other Latin American countries. He bypasses politicians and governmental structures and ensures that the oil reaches the poor directly.

It is not just that oligopolies breed oligopsonies; the converse is also true. While the two words "oligopoly" and "oligopsony" exist in economic vocabulary, there is no economic term that covers the increasingly common scenario of corporations serving as both oligopolies and oligopsonies, i.e., when the same few buyers are also the same few sellers. "Oligonomy" means that companies are an oligopoly towards one group (i.e., farmers) and an oligopsony towards another group (retailers). The only group strong enough to deal with an oligopoly is an oligopsony, which leads then to a multi-tiered oligonomy. Safeway, Kroger and Walmart in the US are an oligopoly to consumers, while to producers/farmers and food brokers they are an oligopsony. Vendors providing ice cream are an oligopsony to dairy farmers and simultaneously an oligopoly to supermarkets. The two huge chocolate companies called Archer-Daniels-Midland and Cargill are an oligopsony to West African farmers, bidding one against the other to get the cheapest price for cocoa beans. Thereafter they become an oligopoly when selling to chocolate manufacturers such as Nestle, Kraft, Mars and Hershey. These four chocolate producers become an oligopsony to cocoa merchants, while simultaneously serving as an oligopoly to cocoa retailers who need their products to sell to the consumers. This inter-layered process becomes a "tiered oligonomy."

Understanding the multi-tiered oligonomies that today permeate the capitalist economic paradigm helps us to understand how the various market layers exploit the two end-layers of each layered tier: the farmers/producers at the beginning of the tier and the consumers/shoppers at the other end. These two end layers have no control and no leverage over the middle layers which comprise the oligopoly and oligopsony. Hence, there is no way for producers and consumers to avoid exploitation. As oligonomies are permeating every sector of the market, including coal, timber and produce, it becomes easier to understand why the common people everywhere, in nation after nation, are bitterly impoverished. In fact, this multi-tiered system described above actually includes many more layers, due to endless outsourcing by corporations as well as due to the fact that in many instances, the wealthiest bankers of the world essentially own the corporations, though their names may not appear on the Board of Directors or anywhere in public.

In contrast to the multi-tiered economy manifested in capitalism, Prout propagates a three-tiered economy. Shrii Sarkar wanted a cooperative commonwealth. However, key industries, such as mining, energy and other large-scale projects need to be controlled and managed by the state or regional government. The aim always would be to place control over key industries at the lowest level of government possible. Businesses that are too small to function as cooperatives and that are not concerned with essential goods and commodities can operate as private enterprises, i.e., with individual ownership. This is what comprises Prout's three-tier economy in a nutshell.

What we have today, however, is untenable. How do we move from the present model of severe exploitation of both farmers and consumers to a just form of economic democracy? Prout envisions local movements of resistance that will work to liberate community economies from corporate and government control. They will compel political and economic change at the local level. This stage of resistance will only succeed if there are multiple movements in towns and villages across the land which are interacting with and supporting one another. If the rights of a community in Dantewada, Chhattisgarh, India are grievously violated, then other communities must step forward and voice their support and demand justice for their oppressed brothers and sisters. Without regional, national and supra-national solidarity, resistance movements will simply be wiped off the map one by one by the corporate-government nexus.

For a larger scale movement, Shrii Sarkar developed a new paradigm of social liberation called Samaja. Samaja refers to the formation of socio-economic units. To create these units, we need to consider whether the people of that area, in the words of Shrii Sarkar, have the "same economic problems, uniform economic potentialities, ethnic similarities, the sentimental legacy of the people, and similar geographical features."

Examples of similar economic problems might refer to lack of markets for local produce, surplus or inadequate labor, communication or transportation problems or lack of irrigation. People in one unit should have the chance for equal or similar economic opportunities so that the wealth inequality gap is gradually reduced. Ethnic similarity should be there among the people of a unit. But also, there should be full scope for each and every ethnic group and sub-group to advance economically. Concrete precautions should be in place so as to prevent the development of racism and communalism. To maintain a common collective psychology there should be commonalities, for example, in language, literature, and cultural traditions and expressions. The people should move together based on certain constructive common sentiments. Similar geographical characteristics should be in place, such as topography, river systems, rainfall and water supply. These are the criteria that will be considered when forming Prout Samajas.

Samajas will fight all sorts of exploitation in the society so as to gain justice for all its members. Here also, movements will need to be started right around the world by following Shrii Sarkar's maxim: "Know the area, prepare the plan and serve the people."

One of the scientific processes of social change is *viplava* or revolution. In the wake of every revolution, radical changes occur in individual and social life, and far-reaching changes take place in the *zeitgeist* of the people. The main factor in revolution is the application of tremendous force to move society forward. Shrii Sarkar says, "Replacing one age by another by crushing exploitation and bringing about a change in the collective psychology within a short period of time through the application of tremendous force is what is called 'revolution'." It requires constant studying and then teaching the common people.

Prout envisions a local to global intellectual revolution. We are defining intellectual revolution here as the process of awakening socio-economic and political consciousness in the people so that they become fully aware of their political, cultural and above all economic rights. At present when the masses suffer, they generally do not know who to blame for their suffering and often end up blaming themselves or worse, local minority populations. How to make people conscious of their rights and demands? Along the lines of Paulo Freire, we need to start study circles everywhere, so that everyone understands (1) their oppression, and (2) the name of their oppressor.

Once the people understand their own oppression and who their oppressor is, it means the entire *zeitgeist* of the people has changed. The minds of the majority of the society will think more and more strongly to revolt against the status quo, which is riddled with staticity and thus brings immense harm to the common people. This will soon turn into a relentless fight against each and every form of exploitation. We will see increasing polarization as benevolent societal forces struggle against malevolent forces; i.e., the wealthy elite who put the masses into so much economic misery. When this mindset is established in the masses, they will begin to identify leaders, great personalities from amongst them, who can lead them with exalted ideas towards a glorious new era of human history. This type of revolution, which affects every aspect of life – political, economic, social, cultural, moral and spiritual – is what Shrii Sarkar has called as nuclear revolution.

Many may wonder as to what revolution has to do with spirituality. History shows that during intense revolutionary struggle (which often becomes a civil war), the revolutionaries as well as the general society become brutalized. By meditating with hate on their enemies during the period of revolutionary struggle (be it intellectual or physical), the revolutionaries develop the same psychology as their oppressors, no matter what their ideological differences might be. This is why a revolution of the human spirit is equally essential, not only for preventing such debasement of humanity during revolutionary struggle, but also to take humanity to higher levels of universalism, morality and love.

An intellectual revolution takes years or decades to be manifested. In contrast, a physical revolution can occur in a very short time. Shrii Sarkar poses the question as to whether the suffering humanity is content to wait for decades or even centuries before genuine change occurs. For example, will the Dalits (lowest caste in India) continue to be murdered for still another century after already more than a thousand years of oppression by higher castes in India? We have to consider whether it is moral that people anywhere should suffer for so long merely because we lack the courage to confront exploitation directly. It is time that the suffering masses unite on the platform of anti-exploitation sentiment and surge forward together in a movement for mass upheaval that will embrace physical revolution as well.

Physical revolution, as per Shrii Sarkar, starts with general physical clash (*shastra*) and progresses to clash with weapons (*astra*). Shrii Sarkar notes that physical revolution involves not only a fight against exploiters but a fight against forces used by exploiters to divide humanity, such as caste, racial, ethnic, religious and national sentiments. While Shrii Sarkar advocated decentralized revolutionary movements in each region (samaja), he foretold in addition that there will be a world revolution. The spread of cosmopolitanism and rapid global communications are sowing the seeds of just such a revolution. More and more people are becoming infused with the sentiment of "One World, One Humanity, One Family.' Shrii Sarkar went even beyond this to envision a cosmic family when human beings begin to move to other planets. This vision of the universe as one family Shrii Sarkar calls the 'Great Universe' (Mahavishva).

The goal of every revolution is peace. Many revolutionary thinkers naively believed that after revolution a utopian peace would automatically evolve. This is because the dominant vision of peace in the world comes from religions that evolved around 2000 years ago. Those religions envisioned a messiah or avatar/buddha who would come and establish an era of perfect peace or paradise in which the lion would sit in friendship with the lamb. All current ideas of peace, even those of so-called scientific socialisms are emotionally rooted in this vision of peace.

In contrast to this fantasy, Shrii Sarkar proposes a dynamic vision of peace as the result of fight. For Shrii Sarkar, true peace or shanti is only in the internal realm when consciousness is elevated by meditation. This higher peace (*para shanti*) is itself the result of a fight against debasing forces in the human psychology. The powerful forces of mental expansion and intense, universal love created by meditation are the *élan vital* of social peace.

By contrast, peace in the external world is relative and dynamic. Social peace for Shrii Sarkar is of two varieties: static peace and sentient peace. Static peace, for example, is the peace of slaves working submissively under their masters. Static peace is inimical to human progress. For Shrii Sarkar, the fight against static peace is the fundamental task of the genuinely 'peaceful person' or 'shanta'. This dharma of the peaceful person is implicit in the very root meaning of the word shanta.[1]* The state achieved by this fight is called sentient peace. Shrii Sarkar warns us that sentient peace is never permanent and, if there is a lack of dynamism and vigilance, society can again degenerate to a more static state. Furthermore, any state of sentient peace in one particular era may be a state of static peace in another era. Hence, social struggle is endless and there will never be a form of static utopia. The need for revolution will arise again and again in human society. This struggle to remove the structural violence, the structural sorrow of a society in the state of static peace, is what PROUT is all about.

Shrii Sarkar says that relief from sorrow or *duhkha* is called *nivrtti*. Millions today want relief from economic sorrow. Corporations in India occupying government-sanctioned Socio-Economic Zones (SEZs) that cause the displacement of millions of helpless human beings will not walk away voluntarily. Resistance is required. Today farmers have begun fighting fiercely for their land. Nandigram, West Bengal was the first armed struggle against SEZs in India. The traditional paradigm of farmer suicides and meek acquiescence appears to be coming to an end. A new era of resistance is beginning that will inspire all victims of SEZs and economic globalization. Their goal is economic peace.

Our own goal must be to provide these victims, who now became the vanguard of the struggle against corporate exploitation, the path to economic peace, the glorious

---

1   * Shrii Sarkar notes that "shanta" (peaceful person) is formed by joining the root verb *sham* with the suffix *kta*. So the primary task of a peaceful person is *shamana*. As Shrii Sarkar says, "A person who fights against the antisocial elements and controls them is said to be doing *shamana*."

Garda Ghista

economic alternative called Prout. Even as Shrii Sarkar handed Prout to us as a powerful weapon (astra), we must likewise offer Prout to these noble warriors, these sweet suffering souls, and say to them, "We cannot bear to see you suffering! Please, here lies the end of your suffering. Here is the solution. Please, share with us your vision, your understanding, of Prout and how it can solve all of our problems, how it can end oppression in the world. Then let us work hand in hand, shoulder to shoulder, to establish Prout!"

The cry, "Peace! Peace!" has become a craze in the world today. Can anything be achieved by such cries? There is no way to establish peace except to fight against the very factors which disturb peace…

Where government servants are strong, static, antisocial individuals maintain a low profile. Then a special kind of peace prevails in a country, and this I call "sentient peace". Where government servants are weak, righteous people bend their heads before the dominant influence of antisocial individuals. This is also a kind of peaceful state, which I call "static peace…" Suppose a particular group of people belonging to a particular region oppress or attack another group of people of the same region or of some other region. In such circumstances, if all others simply remain mute spectators or resort to the path of negotiation, compromise or mutual settlement as the only solution, it should be clearly understood that they are encouraging static peace.

Shrii Prabhat Ranjan Sarkar

Morality

In the path towards establishment of Prout, one fundamental requirement is morality. Rather, one can say that without morality, Prout can never be established. As Shrii Sarkar says, it is the principles of morality which lead one to establishment in the Cosmic state. He has also said that without morality, the Prout cooperative model will not work. Hence, not only is morality required on the spiritual level, to acquire spiritual realization, it is also required on the practical level to manifest the various branches of Prout. It is about every single aspect of life being embedded in moral principles.

The word *niiti,* which is the Sanskrit word for morality, means "that which contains the principle of leading." In other words, morality must provide guidance to people in how to move towards spiritual perfection as well as how to envision and work towards manifesting the dream called a Prout society.

Morality is not a black and white affair, nor can it be manifested in a day. It involves a constant internal and external struggle. Sometimes, we fall down from the path of morality. Then we have to pick ourselves up and try harder the next day. So it is an unending struggle. For some people, a particular aspect of morality, such as taking food only as required, is an easy task. For others, this propensity might be very difficult to control. For some people, jealousy looms large with every step they take. Other people may never feel this propensity. For some people, stealing from others cannot be controlled. For others, they cannot imagine stealing even from their government, even on the very abstract level, so strict they are. How to implement a new economic structure when thousands of common people are robbing the government one way or the other? How can even a Prout government implement welfare schemes for the poor if the people are going to cheat and rob every step of the way?

Shrii Sarkar says, "Morality is a living force, the practice of which makes the mind increasingly contemplative, thereby establishing it in supreme subtlety, in supreme cognition. There is a state from which human beings cannot be led to some other state – the question does not arise. Morality is only worthy of the name if it can inspire human beings to reach that state."

If in a society, let us say in a community or a village, some persons are allowed to steal, or allowed to practice what some call immoral habits such as drinking alcohol, smoking, or sexual promiscuity, those actions on the part of a few affect the entire community, isn't it? It will certainly disturb the collective mental peace. With each of these actions, others are bound to be affected. If a man comes home drunk, he is at some point bound to consider beating up his wife for no reason except that he is out of control. Millions of drunk men do beat up their wives. Is this fair to the poor wives? Hence, it is essential that this immoral behaviour of the man be stopped by the entire community, the entire village. If a man smokes, others seeing him will get the idea to smoke. In millions of cases, smoking leads to cancer and premature death. So if a man smokes, risking premature death, the wife may be left unable to support herself and her children. Is it fair? When he smokes, if his children inhale the smoke he exhales, they stand a high chance of developing leukaemia. Is it fair to the children of that man?

If a man steals from another man, the second man will be furious; there may be a physical fight or a legal case. Is it proper utilization of people's time and energy to spend it in the courts or in physical fights? No. If a man is sexually promiscuous, finally one day his wife will find out, and her happiness will be destroyed forever. Is it fair? If her happiness is destroyed, then what chance do her children have for happiness? Thus with each immoral action, others in the community are compelled to suffer. For this reason, it becomes mandatory for the community to be strict with those who are immoral in any sphere of life. If a man steals the grains stored in an agricultural cooperative, then can the cooperative function properly? If eight out of ten men are stealing grain from a cooperative, can the cooperative function? Of course not. Even suppose that where we find eight men out of ten stealing grain from the cooperative, if we organize for their public flogging or banishment from the town, at least we will be establishing minimum morality. Shrii Sarkar defined minimum social morality as when alcoholism, gambling and prostitution are not present in the society. Without that minimum morality, we cannot establish Prout. Without that minimum morality we cannot build a new world. But, this is our dream, isn't it?

To fight the present immorality, to fight to establish that new moral standard, is a horrendous task. Hardly anyone in the society wants to take on this task. But, the handful of people who do so become great. They become the leaders of the world. They become spiritual revolutionaries. It is the spiritual revolutionaries who, with their heightened discrimination, heightened morality and heightened love gained from their spiritual and intuitional practice, have the courage to remove all sorts of divisive tendencies in themselves and in others. They will have the moral and spiritual capacity to lead others along the path of righteousness.

In the present era, immorality is so rampant that we require a moral revolution in every sphere of life – political, economic, cultural, social, psychological and spiritual. It requires tremendous struggle to oppose immorality in just one sphere of life, and yet we are stating here that we need a complete revolution in the moral standard of the age. Without such a moral revolution, we cannot build a new world. Without such a moral revolution, we cannot establish Prout. Hence, the urgent need of our time is to seek out the individuals who adore morality from the very core of their hearts and who long to live in a moral world. Shrii Sarkar's endless battle cry was, "Moralists of the world unite!" He gave us the mandate. It becomes our task now to seek out the moralists, those who love morality, and unite them on the common platform of fighting all immorality in the society, and fighting economic, political, cultural and religious exploitation. As Shrii Sarkar also said, this is an unending task. The day will never come when the moralists can rest easy and take a vacation. Immoralists and demons never take vacations. Hence, our struggle against immoral forces, both internal and external, is also unending.

During his lifetime, Shrii Sarkar created a moral revolution. While other spiritual leaders welcomed exploitative industrialists, Shrii Sarkar had his followers launch protests against them in Chhattisgarh and other areas. He demanded absolute moral strictness and used his boundless intuitional powers not to become a fortune teller but to maintain the moral integrity of his followers. He used to publicly expose and thrash those followers who took bribes or violated basic moral norms. It generated strong, moral fervour in his disciples, who then themselves demanded morality in their workplaces. It led to Shrii Sarkar quickly attracting many enemies. Idealistic police officers in Bihar, disgusted with the all-pervasive corruption and lawlessness of Indian society, joined Shrii Sarkar's movements in large numbers. In response, the Indian Central Government banned all civil servants from becoming followers of Shrii Sarkar already long before the Indian National Emergency. It was the attraction of the moral power (shakti) of Shrii Sarkar that led the Indian government to file countless fraudulent cases and launch a media campaign against Shrii Sarkar .

Throughout his stay in prison Shrii Sarkar condemned the corruption of jail officials and the government, despite their attempts to assassinate him. As he said, 'I can scold a million people at a time. That is the reason the immoralists cannot stand before me."

From the first expression of moralism, to the establishment in cosmic humanity, there is a gap. The concerted effort to negotiate this gap is termed as social progress, and the collective body of those who are engaged in this concerted effort I shall call the "society."

Shrii Prabhat Ranjan Sarkar

Sadvipras

Shrii Sarkar has created a new paradigm of the revolutionary, which is sadvipra. It means spiritual moralist or spiritual revolutionary. Sadvipras will work to bring about intellectual revolution or to mobilize the exploited masses of a region for physical revolution.

The strong spiritual moralists who fight ceaselessly against immorality, corruption and all forms of injustice in the society are revolutionaries. Shrii Sarkar has introduced a new term for such persons. He calls them "sadvipras." He says, "Sadvipras are those whose all efforts are directed towards the attainment of Bliss. They are strong in morality and always ready to wage war against immoral activities. Those who strictly adhere to the principles of morality, are ensconced in sacrificing service (tapah) and are ready to wage war against immoralists are sadvipras. Only those sadvipras are safe from destruction and extinction who can work for the welfare of the human society. Therefore, it becomes the prime duty of everyone to make themselves and others sadvipras. Shrii Sarkar further says, "Sadvipras will wage a ceaseless, pactless struggle against immorality and all sorts of divisive tendencies. Those who pose to be righteous (dharmic) but are timid with the spirit of fight cannot be called sadvipras."

According to Shrii Sarkar, it is possible for wealthy persons to become sadvipras, but only after they give away most of their wealth. It is not possible to preach about morality to others while living in the lap of luxury, is it? Particularly as in many instances their wealth was acquired on the blood, sweat and tears of the poor. A prime quality of the sadvipra is that they will ceaselessly fight against sin and injustice. The number of persons in any society who engage in the fight against sin and injustice is always relatively small. Hence we can find them rather easily. It is such people alone who should be our leaders. It is such people who will always take care of the oppressed, marginalized, neglected human beings before others, before the middle class persons and certainly before the wealthy persons. These individuals are extra sensitive to suffering. They do not want to see anyone in the society suffering. This extra sensitivity is mandatory to becoming a sadvipra. Those who do not feel this extra sensitivity towards the poor, marginalized, oppressed human beings may like to think that they are sadvipras, but they are not the deciders. It is the oppressed people alone who will decide who are the sadvipras and who they want as their leaders. It is the oppressed people alone who will know who has genuine selfless, omnipotent love for them. Even the poorest, most illiterate person can understand who loves them and how much they love. To define this all-embracing love that we find in the sadvipras, Shrii Sarkar has given the term "Neohumanism."

Today I earnestly request all rational, spiritual, moral, fighting people to build a sadvipra society without any further delay. Sadvipras will have to work for all countries, for the all-round liberation of all human beings. The downtrodden people of this persecuted world look to the eastern horizon, eagerly awaiting their advent. Let the blackness of the new-moon night be lifted from the path of the downtrodden. Let the new human beings of a new day wake up to a new sunrise in a new world.

Shrii Prabhat Ranjan Sarkar

Neohumanism

Material solutions alone cannot solve the problems of humanity. This is because the problems of humanity are often internal, in the form of negative, narrow sentiments. The mission of Neohumanism is to cleanse the collective heart of these narrow forms of love and elevate humanity towards universal love.

Neohumanism is a new zeitgeist propounded by Shrii Prabhat Ranjan Sarkar that we are to love not only our family members, our neighbours, our fellow countrymen; we are to love all the people of this world. Neohumanism goes one step further and says, we are to love even the animals, plants and even the rocks and mountains, and protect them from harm in the best way possible. How are we to reach this neohumanist stance? Neohumanism is not a set of concepts. It is a state of being. Neohumanism is based on the expansion of human consciousness found in mystical practice (meditation) and the intensification of the human heart found in mystical love (bhakti). This mysticism is innate within all cultural traditions. It is this mystical realization which we all share that is the basis for the dynamism of neohumanism.

Based on this expanded consciousness, neohumanism examines and attempts to heal the pathologies of narrow sentiments that distort the human spirit, putting human beings into little boxes of race, class, caste, nation, ethnicity and religion. In addition, neohumanism provides a means for genuine mental liberation from psycho-economic exploitation, that is, the nexus between cultural and economic imperialism. Finally, neohumanism provides a means of regenerating the various sub-cultures of the one culture that is called humanity. It is a mindset that we urgently need because it will help to unite the common people - first to stop the exploitation of the oppressors and then to build a new world based on the universal culture of neohumanism.

Shrii Sarkar warned us even in the 1970s that human beings must live in ecological equilibrium with all aspects of nature so as to protect the precious biodiversity and ecosystem. He believed that humanity is at a crucial juncture, poised between intensifying chaos on the one hand and emerging planetary renaissance on the other. He urged all good people to respond to this predicament by countering the negative forces presently fragmenting, oppressing and exploiting humanity. He wanted those inspired by universal love to struggle vigorously to end humanity's degradation and to unleash its higher physical, intellectual, cultural and spiritual potential to move the human species towards a new realm of consciousness or Neohumanity. This is a revolution in the very nature of what it means to be a human being.

As people become more generous and broad-minded,
they rise above the feelings of casteism, tribalism,
provincialism and nationalism, which evoke
narrowness, violence, hatred and meanness. Those
who enter the field of social welfare with feelings
of "mine" and "yours" actually create divisions
in human society. Those who wish to foster the
welfare of living beings as a whole have to embrace
universalism as the only alternative. If we look upon
everything as our own, the question of "mine" and
"yours" will dissolve; in universalism there is no
opportunity for violence, hatred or narrowness.

Shrii Prabhat Ranjan Sarkar

Zeitgeist of the 21st Century

One of the important programs started by Shrii Sarkar is called sadavrata – the eternal vow to serve all. This vow is manifested primarily by feeding the people. Shrii Sarkar also said that the very first work of Proutists is to feed the people. If people are hungry, are starving, they are not in a position to absorb new ideas and ideals. They are also not in a position to study economic theories and compare and contrast capitalism, communism and Prout. So first, we must feed the hungry and the starving.

However, it is not about feeding the people. This is not the larger goal. It is the smaller goal. The larger goal is to create a love revolution in the society. It means, to create in all human beings the desire, the longing, to feed the hungry people. Just imagine, if in your town, 90 percent of the people spent two hours every morning cooking tasty, healthy food and took it out to the hungry people in their neighbourhood and fed them. Can we not call that a revolution? A revolution in the collective mindset of the people? This is the larger goal, brothers and sisters. Feeding the people is the immediate, urgent, but smaller goal. It is just one step in the march to creating a world where people have so much love for their fellow human beings that it will become unthinkable for even one person to go hungry. This is called changing the zeitgeist of the era. This was the mission of Shrii Prabhat

Ranjan Sarkar. He showed us the dream. Now we need to manifest that dream.

Recently in New York City a man began attacking a woman. A second man came and rescued her. But, the attacker stabbed him repeatedly in the chest and ran away. The courageous man ran after the attacker but fell down in the last throes of life. For one hour, nobody helped him. Twenty five pedestrians walked past him, some looked, others pushed his body a bit to see the problem. But nobody phoned the ambulance for one hour, and by that time he lay dead, a silent hero and a living testimony to man's indifference to his fellow man. We need to change this.

Shrii Sarkar did say in this regard that during the era of the Mahabharata, it was unthinkable for people to allow a single person to go hungry. Please contrast that era with today. He also said that when famine approached the kingdom of the great King Chandragupta, he gave away all his food and wealth to save his people from starvation. When the ministers objected, he said," When everybody is dying, I will also die." Three days later his body was found under a tree. Do we have a leader like this today? In every community there exist these stories, these tales, of supreme sacrifice. To inaugurate a renaissance, a love revolution, to restore the lost sublimity of humanity, is what Shrii Prabhat Ranjan Sarkar is all about. Please, let us start a love revolution today. Let us all feed the starving people today. Let it today become unthinkable that a single human being go hungry or be homeless. Let us build a new world on the ashes of the old.

Let your advent in this world be successful in all ways. I want your existence to shine, to be resplendent with the joy of being alive. This is the reason why I introduced … sadávrata – to bring supreme fulfillment to your lives. Let your advent on this earth be successful, individually and collectively.

Shrii Prabhat Ranjan Sarkar

Other Contributions

"History moves in rhythmic waves – in a systaltic flow. It moves and moves, then there is a galloping jump. Again it moves and moves again, then there is another galloping jump, and so on. All of a sudden there are galloping jumps – epoch-making eras. We are now at the threshold of this jump. We are not only at the threshold, we have just crossed the threshold of a new era. We are now at the threshold of something new – of the new age – and we are now passing through such an age. Do you realize it? We are no more at the threshold. You should be ready for great changes, otherwise balance will be lost. In the process of movement, there cannot be steady movement. There must be acceleration – either constant acceleration or accelerated acceleration – or retardation – either constant retardation or retarding retardation. Along with this acceleration or retardation, there is a galloping jump. Before and after this jump, there is biological change, historical change, agricultural change and human psychic change."

Shrii Prabhat Ranjan Sarkar

To prepare humanity for these great, epoch-making changes on earth, Shrii Sarkar initiated numerous plans and programs to accelerate this process. These are just a few areas in which he instilled revolutionary ideas to propel the society forward at a rapid pace, to leap into the future.

Education

Shrii Prabhat Ranjan Sarkar created a new vision for education in the world, to include daily yoga exercises, kiirtana and meditation. In addition the curriculum is to include incorporation of the neohumanist mindset, such that every child from young age learns to love not just his family, not just his community, not just his own town, but the entire world. World geography would be a mandatory subject every year, so as to bring the children of one region intimately close to the children of another region on the other side of the globe, and would include all types of exchange programs to enhance the feeling of universalism in all. The children would be taught to love not only human beings but also their friends and neighbours, the birds and animals, and would even learn to treat all inanimate objects with respect.

The schools of Shrii Sarkar are about inculcating a deeper, higher value system in the children. When curricula for such schools are spread around the world, casteism would become a barbaric relic in the history museum, women's oppression would end as boys learn from birth to respect and adore their mothers, wives, sisters and daughters. Hatred for people of other communities and religions would come to a blissful end as children are instead filled with an ocean of devotion to the Lord and His glorious manifestations, as represented by entire humanity.

The visionary educational system developed by Shrii Sarkar is already being used in more than 200 schools in Africa and over 1,000 schools in South Asia. Before his departure, he laid the groundwork and guidelines for creating a university or Gurukula, which again would emphasize fundamental human rights and justice for all. The goal of every educated citizen must be to liberate the oppressed of the world and work ceaselessly towards creating an ideal society where "oppression" becomes an unknown word not even to be found in the dictionary.

Regarding education, Shrii Sarkar said, "To make people conscious of their rights in every sphere of life – social, economic, psychic and spiritual – is called the expansion of knowledge; and to exercise these rights fully is called the cultivation of science. Neglected people, who have remained ignorant of different branches of knowledge for whatever reason, should be given maximum opportunities to develop. There should not be any discrimination as far as these rights are concerned. ....We cannot build a strong society if we discriminate against a section of humanity by drawing imaginary lines of distinction between the educated and the uneducated. People must develop closer and closer links with each other. One heart must gain a warm and deep understanding of another heart."

Animal Rights

Today thousands of chickens are stacked in crates and left in the summer sun to die. Pigs lie dead of heart attacks in slaughterhouses, or with their heads trapped firmly in a gate, moaning in misery. Men arrive regularly with heavy boots and electric prods, causing the pigs to erupt in screams until finally they lose consciousness and are saved only by death. Butchers say that hogs provoke their violence by being obstinate. But the reality is that the hogs sense completely what is going to happen to them and are terrified for their lives. Male baby chickens are of no use to anyone in the poultry business. Consequently they are weeded out and dropped into heavy plastic bags to suffocate to death. Female chickens allowed to live are kept in unbelievably cramped conditions such that sometimes their webbed feet grow around the cage wires. Invariably they are "de-beaked", which entails cutting off part of their beaks, a severely painful process that often results in their being unable to drink.

There is a crying need to publicize the plight of animals in all countries of the world - animals which undergo totally unnecessary physical and mental suffering at the hands of human beings who, because they are addicted to feeding on their flesh, cause them agonizing physical pain and mental anguish. Not enough is said about this today anywhere except in a few select books on the topic of animal rights. In a compassion-based society, this should be a topic of number one importance. The slightest cruelty to even one cow, sheep, goat, pig or chicken should not be tolerated by the society as a whole.

Shrii Prabhat Ranjan Sarkar told us clearly that before killing birds and animals for food, we must think hundred times whether we can stay alive without killing them. In a future charter of rights inculcating his ideas, Shrii Sarkar stipulated that the first and most important principle will be to guarantee complete security to all plants and animals. Hence, with these words of his reverberating in our hearts, it becomes the mandate of us all to dedicate our lives to promoting the inalienable rights of animals to live out their natural lives in peace and security, and to expose violations of these rights. No one has the moral right to kill any animal except in life-threatening circumstances.

To further this goal, in 1977 Shrii Sarkar formed the organization called PCAP – Prevention of Cruelty to Animals and Plants. Since its inception PCAP has grown to become a global movement. Some of its goals include prevention of cruelty to animals, birds, plants and trees; protecting rare and dying species from extinction; preventing deforestation so as to maintain ecological equilibrium; creating a sentiment of love for animals, birds and plants in popular culture; popularizing vegetarianism so as to save the lives of innocent animals and birds; providing food to animals and building sanctuaries so that they can be given medical treatment and live in security, particularly in their old age.

In 1988 Shrii Sarkar started a second project called PASAKA', which stands for Parivesh Samvardhana Ka'nana or "Garden for the Development of All Living Beings." It began as a refuge and sanctuary for rare and endangered plants and animals and as an environmental legacy for the once extensive forests and unique wildlife that covered the Indian subcontinent. PASAKA is located in a twelve square mile area called Ananda Nagar (City of Bliss) which was envisioned by Shrii Sarkar as a multi-faceted development model for rural regeneration and economic self-sufficiency based on moral and spiritual values. This area, bordering the states of West Bengal and Jharkhand in eastern India, is one of the poorest and ecologically devastated zones of the Indian subcontinent.

Women's Liberation

The liberation of women is one of the most important goals of Shrii Sarkar. Women have been oppressed, suppressed and repressed over centuries. They have not been allowed to speak, to work or to develop intellectually. Recently in Bangladesh women have again been banned from participating in any sports. In other Muslim countries horrific honour killings abound. And in India violence towards women is number one, as dowry deaths occur by the thousands, and female foeticide and infanticide take place in the millions. Acid attacks committed equally by both Hindu and Muslim men are the greatest disgrace on the South Asian subcontinent. Trafficking and ensuing slavery of women is rampant all over India and adjacent countries.

In the United States four women are killed every day by their spouses, while thousands more lie in hospital emergency rooms with broken jaws and beaten to a pulp. Beyond that millions remain mentally subjugated by coercive, controlling husbands. How many women in every country of the world weep silently in their bed at night, wondering why nobody comes to rescue them from psychological torture meted out by the men in their lives? As documented in innumerable sociology and social work textbooks, the physical suffering meted out to women can be forgotten. But the psychological torture leaves them with invisible wounds and disabilities that can take decades to heal. During times of economic hardship and depression, all these statistics regarding abuse of wives rise exponentially. Hence, fighting against economic depression involves not only creating new economic programs. It also involves a new level of deep caring for all mothers, sisters, daughters and especially wives in our communities, so that together we protect them and each other from new levels of male brutality.

We need to support the fight for women's liberation in all spheres - physical, intellectual and spiritual - and offer moral support to all other organizations that work towards these goals. It is time for women to become free of their shackles, free of those men who consider them as nothing but chattel, free also of those men who, with their constant surveillance, engage in what Dr. Evan Stark calls coercive control.

Dowry is the ancient custom in India where the bride's parents are compelled to give large sums of money to the groom. Due to poverty, due to the unbounded greed of men and their mothers, countless wives in India commit suicide, unable to bear the mental torture of endless demands for more dowry which continue into the marriage. Millions of murders of wives have been carried out by husbands or mother-in-laws because the wife did not bring more money for the husband. For this very reason, parents do not want daughters and more than one million female babies are murdered annually, either upon birth or while still in the womb. The result is that the sex ratios in several states of India are skewed with a sharply higher population level of males. Shrii Sarkar stopped all dowry practice amongst his followers. If anyone accepted or gave dowry, he would ostracize them. He also banned his followers from eating food at weddings where dowry had been given.

Shrii Sarkar also started Nari Abhyudaya, which means "women's awakening." It was a movement that spread rapidly during his lifetime and was driven by two main goals: all women should be educated and all women should be economically self-reliant. In addition he created Women's Welfare Department (WWD) to create schools and homes for orphans and centers for service to women. Shrii Sarkar founded still another organization called Girls' Proutists so as to make young women the leaders of the Prout movement. He created Girls' Volunteers (GV) with the mandate to train young women to fight against corruption and women's oppression. He mandated two educational faculties to be a part of every future university: the Faculty of Women's Economic Liberation and the Faculty of Women's Liberation. One was to provide programs to make poor women economically independent and the other was to work for women's total liberation worldwide.

It is time for women to break free and to now itself become the leaders of the world. In the words of Shrii Sarkar, "We stand to create a powerful, dynamic and upsurging social consciousness, especially among women, so that they are inspired to rise, abolish dogma and annihilate all symbols of slavery, and usher in a new era of coordinated cooperation and glorious achievement. Let women be the vanguard of a new revolution which humanity must achieve for a glorious tomorrow."

A Casteless Society

Casteism is the oldest form of prejudice in human history. Arising from the racism of the invading Aryans, as seen in the Vedas, casteism has become the defining element of Indian social life. Just as the world took action and protested against the inhumane system of apartheid, similarly the world must now take action and protest against the barbaric caste system in India. Ridding India of casteism would not only be a giant step forward for India but a giant step forward for humanity. It is the Prout mandate to support all efforts to rid the world of the scourge of casteism.

Shrii Sarkar stated boldly that "those who imposed

the caste system were wicked, crooked demons." In his determination to rid Indian society of casteism, he encouraged revolutionary marriages, defined as marriage between persons of two entirely different castes, races or nations. This vision met with fierce resistance during his lifetime. Today it has become somewhat normal for men and women of differing upper castes to intermarry. But still, the gap between upper and lower castes remains as large as ever. And still, the unbounded arrogance of upper castes is intact as they alone demand perpetuation of the caste system, which puts them in a favourable position in the society. They continue to deny the atrocities committed against the lower castes, and even simply the horrors of living in India as an untouchable.

For the lower castes, particularly the Dalits or untouchables, their lives remain a kind of hell on earth. Dalit women are routinely raped by barbaric policemen, while upper caste men keep them as mistresses. Dalit men are routinely lynched, with the highest statistics coming from West Bengal. Most recent studies indicate that Dalits in India are attacked by higher caste men every 20 minutes every single day. Shrii Sarkar said, "You will have to remove all distinctions based on caste. So the caste system itself must be eradicated. Removing different types of disparities comes within either the socio-economic, psychic or spiritual approaches. In this case the social disparity of casteism comes within the realm of PROUT."

Philology

Philology, in the vision of Shrii Prabhat Ranjan Sarkar, begins with traditional philological fields, such as textual philology, comparative philology and cognitive philology. His vision goes on to embrace related fields of phonetics and linguistics, with special emphasis on phonosemantics. The holistic philology of Shrii Sarkar embraces also the fields of ecology, medicine, agriculture, history, the arts, philosophy, Tantra, and mysticism. Indeed, for Shrii Sarkar, philology embraces every aspect of human existence.

He extended the expressive range of the Bengali language by adding approximately 18,000 words to its vocabulary. He made its script more systematic by adding several letters to its alphabet and recommended similar changes to other Indian languages. He also wrote grammar texts for English as well as for the neglected, oppressed languages of Bihar. One of the major projects of his later years was the dictation of an encyclopaedia on Bengali, Sanskrit and other Indian languages and cultures.

Through these philological explorations, Shrii Sarkar was in fact creating a cultural revolution in the Bengali language. In the tradition of Indian social movements, such as the Sufi and bhakti movements throughout Indian history, the élan vital is culture. Shrii Sarkar notes how in India's past all of the arts and humanities were based on mysticism. Traditional Indian philology is based on the spiritual practices of Tantra, which serve as a basis for the expansion of the microcosm into the macrocosm. Traditional western philology is based on the historical analysis of texts that serve as the foundation for socio-political identity. Shrii Sarkar unites both approaches to serve as the vehicle for ecological, linguistic, social, economic and political revolution. Again, this holistic revolution is what Prout is all about.

Shrii Sarkar wanted that every human being have

the right to learn in their mother language. Hence he mandated that every national constitution protect and nurture every language in its domain, regardless of the size of population speaking that language today. Throughout the developing world, indigenous peoples are subject to physical, economic and cultural genocide. Shrii Sarkar emphasized that many indigenous communities are in fact more civilized, with less violence and no castes or classes, than so-called advanced cultures. In fact, the majority of Prout programs are simply a renaissance and modernization of indigenous ideals and cultures. Hence, as Proutists, we seek to study the culture behind progressive, indigenous, ecological, economic and social practices and endeavour to propagate them in the society. This is what Shrii Sarkar envisioned as Neohumanist philology, in which the flowering of linguistic diversity strengthens the unity of humanity. Shrii Sarkar spoke fluently in over 200 languages and had command of most linguistic scripts. Though demonstrating knowledge of so many languages and dialects, Shrii Sarkar insisted that in fact, he knew only one language – the language of the heart.

Prabhata Samgiita

Shrii Sarkar composed 5018 songs in just eight years. Singing these songs takes one into so many realms, from love of the streams and rivers to the fight against injustice and still further into the depths of devotional tenderness. Tenderness is the hallmark, the keynote, of Prabhata Samgiita. This tenderness is not the child-like tenderness that only partly melts the heart. The tenderness in these songs can be defined as *teneritas tremendum* - "overwhelming tenderness," like a tsunami of tenderness.

When one is faced with something awesomely intense that staggers the body and mind, it is called "*tremendum.*" When faced with a softness that pours into the core of one's yearning heart, it is called "*teneritas.*" To synthesize these two cardinal dimensions of human experience is the genius of Shrii Prabhat Ranjan Sarkar.

What Neohumanism and especially Prabhata Samgiita both do are to express this tenderness more profoundly in the vast arena of the entire cosmos and beyond into the realm of mystical love. Finally, this tenderness expands to fill each and every act and struggle of our daily lives and every small service to humanity, transforming those lives into a veritable song of love. This is indeed the triumph of tenderness for which humanity's heart has yearned since it first took birth on earth. Through these songs of the new dawn, Prabhata Samgiita, the author has inaugurated the dawn of a genuinely righteous and sublime society. The name "Prabhat Ranjan Sarkar" literally means, "the lord who colours the dawn."

In Indian history, the events that had the maximum impact on society were the bhakti and Sufi movements, in which the force of mystical love expressed in devotional songs and kiirtana was able to create a profound stir in the society, and whose impact is still with us today. In Iran, Turkey and other countries, Sufi poets transformed their societies through their poetry of mystical love Through the sublimely sweet songs called Prabhata Samgiita, Shrii Sarkar has laid the foundation for a global renaissance of the devotional movement, for a revolution of devotional love. It is this devotional revolution that is the heartbeat of the Prout revolution.

These shackles of vice,
This fortress of corruption
Break free and pulverize them.
Come brothers and sisters,
Come with an open heart,
Merging with everyone.
Do not stay away anymore.
Break free and pulverize them.
Demons are tyrannizing and exploiting,
Guarding and nourishing their gangsters.
The vicious and the depraved revel in joy,
While the helpless poor are frantic.
Break free and pulverize them.
O look at the colourful sun
In the eastern skies.
Wipe out all the piled-up darkness;
See to it that the sun doesn't sink.
And that demons do not prowl in the dark.
Break free and pulverize them.

Shrii Prabhat Ranjan Sarkar
Prabhata Samgiita 4871

Infinite Humility and Incorrigible Optimism

Prout is just one facet of the multi-dimensional, multi-disciplinary contributions given to the world by Shrii Prabhat Ranjan Sarkar. It will be correct to state that Shrii Sarkar was the renaissance man of the 20th century and beyond, as history will surely reveal. He demonstrated over and over that the ultimate human fulfilment comes from attaining mystical merging with the Supreme. He combined deep love and samadhi with a profound commitment to life and to suffering humanity, and challenged all dogmas that suppress the liberation of human beings. On the one hand he gave exquisite poetic expression to humanity's nobler sentiments, and on the other hand he encouraged active and pauseless struggle against the forces of oppression and exploitation. Shrii Sarkar inspired his followers to work tirelessly to create a societal revolution - a political, economic, cultural, moral and spiritual revolution.

His motivation for socio-economic and political struggle was rooted in his unbounded love and compassion for suffering humanity. In addition, he worked without pause to serve the downtrodden, starving, neglected, half-naked people of the world, teaching his followers that service to suffering humanity is service to the Lord. He gave the concept that when we serve we are not to expect thanks from anyone. Rather, when we serve we are to thank the Lord again and again for giving us the beautiful opportunity to perform that service. Taking it one step further, he told us that instead we are to abandon entirely the vanity of performing any service. We should feel that any service we do is being performed by the Lord.

Shrii Sarkar lived a life of simplicity, and conducted his personal affairs with virtue and decorum, behaving in a manner consistent with his beliefs. He refused to become a public personality, avoiding all contact with the media or the curious public. In 1986, he used to invite people on a tour of his garden. At the beginning of those tours, he would come and humbly thank everyone for coming to see his garden. His words were the epitome of humility, the epitome of courtesy and politeness, of sublime charm and benevolence. In his every move, every gesture, every word, and every tone and accent when speaking any word, he was setting an example of how to be in this world, of how to be a true gentleman.

Shrii Sarkar never believed in fate; his slogan was "Fight against fate." He said that we determine our fate by our own deeds and actions. He scolded those who sometimes used to read books of astrology and palmistry. He said that in the life of the activist, these things should never be encouraged. If an astrologer gave a gloomy prediction to any of his followers, he would ask them to prove the astrologer wrong. Not only that, he would demand that they do something truly tremendous to prove the astrologer wrong – and create triumph out of disaster.

Shrii Sarkar defined himself as an incorrigible optimist. Even in the darkest of times, he emboldened us all in words that speak to us today. He said, "You do your work. All will be settled well. There is no reason for one to fear at the sight of a dead horse. But certainly one would run away seeing a living lion. Similarly, immoralists are afraid of us - so roar like a lion!"

Telling the world about the astounding achievements of Shrii Sarkar does little to illuminate the greatness of the man behind those achievements. He radiated a profound sense of mission to promote liberation in its fullest sense. When in good health, and even when in poor health, he worked twenty hours a day, seven days a week, to elevate and liberate humanity via countless service programs. To manifest the ideals of PROUT practically, he guided the development of bioregional movements (Samajas) and sustainable communities for economic freedom and self-reliance. The depth of his commitment to justice for all beings proved irresistible to thousands, who visited him from continents around the world just to experience his infinite love, compassion, mercy and magnanimity. For centuries to come, humanity will tell touching, tender stories about this mysterious man whose name was Shrii Prabhat Ranjan Sarkar.

To understand my nature you must do meditation. I keep no ambiguity. Do you know what ambiguity is? Ambiguity means many things. But I keep no ambiguity. I am clear, concrete, conclusive. My philosophy is a complete philosophy – a complete way of life. I am complete in myself and I want every person to be complete in himself and herself. I am like an arrow, clear, pointed.

Shrii Prabhat Ranjan Sarkar

About the Author

Garda Ghista is author of *The Gujarat Genocide: A Case Study in Fundamentalist Cleansing* and *Wife Abuse: Breaking It Down and Breaking Out*. She is also Founding President of World Prout Assembly, an organization to raise consciousness in every sphere of life, and more recently of Hearts Healing Hunger, which has the sole mandate to feed the hungry people everywhere. The work of feeding the hungry has already begun in North Bengal, India. If you can help in any way, please contact her at gardaghista@gmail.com.